The Pinckney Treaty

America Wins the Right to Travel the Mississippi River

Holly Cefrey

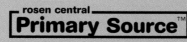

rosen central
Primary Source™

The Rosen Publishing Group Inc., New York

To the Oguma family

Published in 2004 by The Rosen Publishing Group, Inc.
29 East 21st Street, New York, NY 10010

First Edition

Library of Congress Cataloging-in-Publication Data

Cefrey, Holly.
The Pinckney Treaty: America wins the right to travel the Mississippi River / by Holly Cefrey. — 1st ed.
   p. cm. — (Life in the new American nation)
Summary: Describes how this treaty, also known as the Treaty of San Lorenzo, came to be signed in 1795 by the United States and Spain, and how the agreement allowed America to grow westward and to avoid war with Spain.
Includes bibliographical references (p.) and index.
ISBN 0-8239-4041-1 (lib.bdg.)
ISBN 0-8239-4259-7 (pbk.bdg.)
6-pack ISBN 0-8239-4272-4
1. San Lorenzo Treaty, 1795—Juvenile literature. 2. United States—Foreign relations—Spain—Juvenile literature. 3. Spain —Foreign relations—United States—Juvenile literature. 4. Mississippi River Valley—History—To 1803—Juvenile literature. [1. San Lorenzo Treaty, 1795. 2. United States—Foreign relations—Spain. 3. Spain—Foreign relations—United States. 4. Mississippi River Valley—History—To 1803.] I. Title. II. Series.
E313.C43 2003
327.73046—dc21

2002153794

Manufactured in the United States of America

Cover (left): map of the Mississippi River from Cairo to its mouth in 1863
Cover (right): portrait of Don Manuel de Godoy on the battlefield by Francisco de Goya y Lucientes

Photo credits: cover (left), pp. 1, 11, 15 © Library of Congress; cover (right), p. 23 © Archivo Iconografico, S.A./Corbis; p. 4 © Hulton/Archive/Getty Images; p. 7 © Department of the Interior/American Political History; p. 9 © American Political History; p. 13 © Corbis; p. 19 © National Archives and Records Administration; p. 25 © Bettmann/Corbis.

Designer: Nelson Sá; Editor: Eliza Berkowitz; Photo Researcher: Nelson Sá

Contents

Introduction

The Pinckney Treaty is known by many names. The proper name of the treaty is the Treaty of Friendship, Limits, and Navigation Between Spain and the United States. It is also known simply as the Treaty of Friendship. It has also been called the Treaty of San Lorenzo. San Lorenzo is the Spanish village where the treaty was signed. Other names for it are the Treaty of 1795 and Pinckney's Treaty. All

This is a portrait of Thomas Pinckney from the 1790s. It is an engraving done by W. G. Armstrong from a miniature in oil by J. Trumbull. Pinckney is best remembered for his negotiation of the Pinckney Treaty.

these names describe a single important treaty in American history.

A treaty is an agreement between the governments of two or more countries. The Pinckney Treaty was an agreement between Spain and the early American government. The agreement was made between two people. These people were representatives, or officials, of America and Spain. They were Thomas Pinckney and Don Manuel de Godoy.

They worked together to make a document. A document is a paper with written facts. Documents often list rules that countries will follow. When a government accepts the rules of a document, the document becomes law.

The Pinckney Treaty is important because it allowed America to grow westward. This was during a time when much of America was a vast wilderness. Foreign governments claimed rule over parts of America. Spain was one of the governments that made claims in America. A claim is the demand of ownership over something such as land. Many claims on American land caused wars. Pinckney's treaty was made to help America and Spain avoid war with each other.

Chapter 1

Early America—Discovering the Future

The Pinckney Treaty was made in the late 1700s. America was very different back then. Settlers came from many parts of Europe. They came to build a new life in America. Most settlers lived in the early American colonies. The colonies were located along the eastern part of North America. As more settlers came, America began to expand and grow westward.

America was discovered by Europeans in the 1400s. Countries such as Spain and France wanted to explore and build colonies in America. America was valuable because it had many resources. New land, plants, lumber, and furs were among the many resources in America.

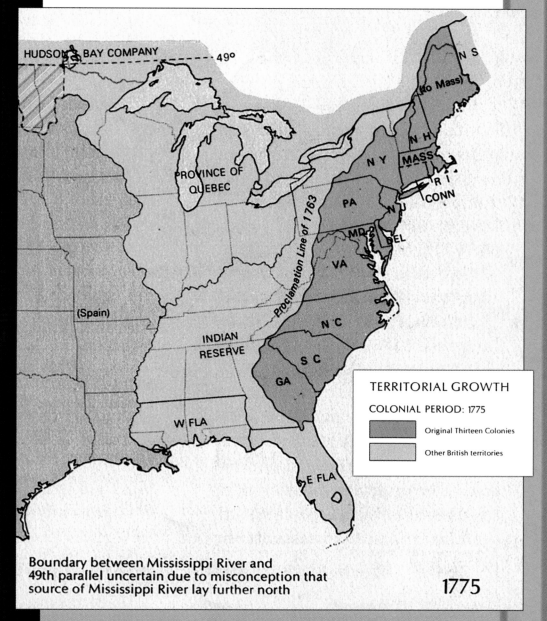

HUDSON BAY COMPANY — 49°

N S

(to Mass)

N H

N Y — MASS

PROVINCE OF QUEBEC

R I

CONN

PA

N J

MD

DEL

Proclamation Line of 1763

VA

(Spain)

N C

INDIAN RESERVE

S C

GA

W FLA

E FLA

TERRITORIAL GROWTH

COLONIAL PERIOD: 1775

Original Thirteen Colonies

Other British territories

Boundary between Mississippi River and
49th parallel uncertain due to misconception that
source of Mississippi River lay further north

1775

This map shows how land in the continental United States was divided in 1775. The original thirteen colonies are states that still exist to this day. Most of this land used to belong to Spain and England but is now a part of the United States of America.

At first, Spain said that it was the only country allowed to make land claims in America. Spain built colonies in Florida. The French traveled down the Mississippi River from the Great Lakes. They made land claims on both sides of the Mississippi River. When a country claimed an area of American land, the land fell under that country's rule. Problems and wars broke out in America and Europe over American land claims. Many of these problems were solved by making treaties.

In the 1700s, France claimed a huge piece of land in America. It was between the Rocky Mountains and the Mississippi River. It reached south to the Gulf of Mexico. It reached north to Canada. France also claimed areas east of the Mississippi River.

New Orleans became the official capital of the French land in 1722. New Orleans became important because it was a busy port. A port city is a place where ships load and unload passengers and goods. Many goods from different places can be bought and sold there. In early New Orleans, a ship could travel north up the Mississippi to reach vast resources. A ship could also sail out to sea from the Gulf of Mexico. It became a gateway for America.

France and England were at war from 1754 to 1763. Spain sided with France. France gave New Orleans and the territory west of the Mississippi River to Spain. England won the war and took control of the rest of French land and the Spanish territory of Florida.

During the mid-1700s, England controlled the American colonies. Many of the colonists were unhappy with England's rule. Many of them did not want to have a king. They wanted their own government.

The colonists declared independence in 1776. But England was not willing to give America up. The colonists went to war with England. This war is known as the Revolutionary War, or the War of Independence.

John Jay was a founding father of the United States. Although he did not succeed in making a treaty with Spain in 1780, he negotiated the Jay Treaty in 1794. This was an agreement between the United States and Great Britain.

Americans had hoped that Spain would fight on their side. An American representative named John Jay was sent to Spain in 1780. The American government tried to make a deal with Spain for more than two years. They hoped to arrange a treaty of friendship with Spain. The treaty would declare that Florida would be Spain's forever. In exchange, Spain would support the American claim of independence. Spain would accept the new American government as separate from England. Americans would also be allowed to use the Mississippi River. In addition, Spain was also asked to loan a great deal of money to the American war effort. Unfortunately, the Spanish government did not make a deal with Jay. Spain wanted to protect its own land in America without getting involved in the war between America and England.

The American colonists won the war against England in 1783. The settlers became American citizens. These citizens made a new government. It was also formed to help America grow into a strong, independent country. The government wanted to protect its people while America grew westward.

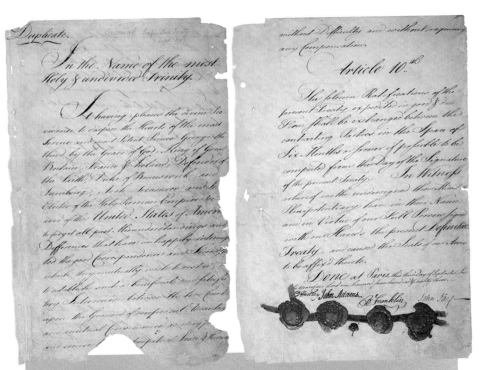

This is the Treaty of Paris. It is also called the Peace Treaty because it brought peace by ending the fighting between the United States, Spain, France, the Netherlands, and England. It also signaled the end of the American War for Independence and established the United States as an independent nation.

Spain fought its own war with England in America. Spain conquered the English in Florida in 1783. The Revolutionary War ended about the same time. The war ended with the signing of the Treaty of Paris, or the Peace Treaty.

Chapter 2   Treaties and Troubles

The Treaty of Paris listed the land that belonged to the colonists. The treaty stated that the southern border of American land was the 31st parallel. The 31st parallel would be the border between America and Florida. England also signed a separate treaty of peace with Spain. It gave Florida back to the Spanish. This treaty did not list the borders of the actual land.

The Treaty of Paris also allowed the Americans and English to use the Mississippi River. The Mississippi River was important because it allowed access into many parts of America. It also connected to New Orleans and the Gulf of Mexico. The western part of America could be

This is a map of the United States in 1783, after independence. It shows how the Treaty of Paris affected the newly independent country. People were settling west of the original thirteen colonies. This began disputes between the United States and Spain over land.

reached from the Mississippi River. Goods could also be shipped from the Gulf of Mexico to Europe and other places. The English hoped to continue to explore American lands by using the Mississippi River.

After the Revolutionary War, America grew and prospered. Americans explored and settled farther west from the original thirteen states. Americans were settling very close to Spanish territories.

Western settlers began to send goods such as lumber back east. Goods were shipped using the Ohio and Mississippi Rivers, and the Gulf of Mexico. New Orleans became a very busy port city. Americans bought and sold goods there.

Spain was unhappy with the Treaty of Paris between England and America. When Florida was under English rule, its northern border was above the 32nd parallel. The border separated the American and English territories. When the land was given back to Spain, the Spanish accepted this northern border.

The Treaty of Paris changed the borderline. It made the border at the 31st parallel. This gave more than 100 miles of Spanish land to the Americans. Spain did not want to lose this land.

On June 29, 1784, Spain claimed a large area of American land. Spain asserted that their northern Florida border was 110 miles north of the 31st parallel.

This map of the Mississippi River is an engraving done by Nicholas King from around 1811. The Mississippi River was very useful because goods such as lumber could be shipped from the west all the way to the southern United States. The Mississippi River is the second longest river in the United States.

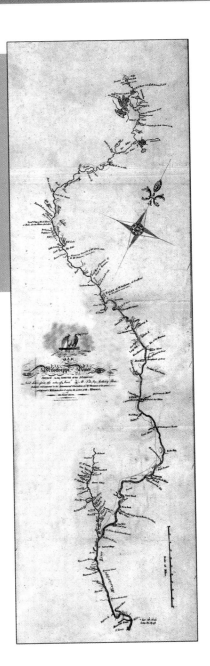

Spain claimed land between the Mississippi and Flint Rivers (land that is now Alabama and Mississippi). This land did not belong to the Americans yet. Native American tribes such as the Creek and the Crow lived in this territory. The Spanish traded goods with the Native Americans.

In 1784, Spain also stopped Americans from using the Mississippi River. Americans were not allowed to go to New Orleans or the Gulf of Mexico. The Spanish would not allow Americans to use these areas until the argument over the border was resolved.

Life without using the river and the port was very hard. Goods had to be sent back and forth by land. Using the river and port was the easiest way to help America grow. The American government was worried about this problem. The government was also worried about having Spanish territories on its southern and western borders.

For ten years following the Treaty of Paris, the Spanish and Americans argued over land. They also tried to make treaties with the Native Americans living in the Alabama and Mississippi territory. Officials from both parties could not reach any agreements. Fortunately, Thomas Pinckney became part of the peace process.

An American with a Purpose

Chapter 3

Thomas Pinckney was no ordinary American. He came from an early founding family. Founding families worked and fought to help America grow as a new nation.

Thomas Pinckney was born in 1750 in Charleston, South Carolina. His mother, Elizabeth Lucas, was a plantation owner. Her father left South Carolina in 1739 to serve the British government. He was stationed in the West Indies. Elizabeth was a teenager when he left. She took control of her father's plantations.

Elizabeth's father mailed some seeds from the West Indies. They were indigo plant seeds. Indigo dye is made from these tropical plants.

President George Washington met Elizabeth Pinckney, Thomas's mother, once when he was touring the South. When Elizabeth died, President Washington asked to be a pallbearer at her funeral. The president honored Elizabeth Pinckney by helping to carry her casket.

Indigo dye was used for many purposes, including fabric dyeing. Elizabeth grew the indigo plants in America. She taught other planters how to grow them. Soon the whole colony was making money from the plants and indigo dye.

Elizabeth married Charles Pinckney. He had a daughter named Harriot from a previous marriage. Elizabeth and Charles had two sons, named Charles Cotesworth and Thomas. (Thomas also had a cousin named Charles, who was also a well- known political leader.) When her husband died in 1758, Elizabeth continued to control the plantations for more than thirty years by herself.

Thomas Pinckney went to London, England, to attend Westminster School. He was an excellent student. He graduated from Oxford University. He then spent a year at Caen, a military school in Normandy, France. He also studied law at Inner Temple in London.

Charles Pinckney, Thomas's cousin, was also involved in government. He was the youngest delegate at the Constitutional Convention and played a major role in revising the Articles of Confederation.

A few English officials already knew Pinckney from his school days. One of these friends told the English Parliament (government), "We have a new American minister, Mr. Pinckney, an old friend and brother Westminster of mine, whose manners and temper exactly qualify him for the place he has taken. I do not know a more worthy and excellent man."

Pinckney missed America while he was in Europe. He was nicknamed "little rebel" because he was a proud American. He returned to Charleston in 1774 and became a lawyer. He married Elizabeth Motte in 1779.

Even though Pinckney was educated in England, he had great hopes for American independence from England. He fought in the Revolutionary War from 1775 to 1781. He fought in battles in Florida and South Carolina. He was shot in the leg during a battle at Camden, South Carolina, and was taken prisoner. He was a prisoner for more than a year in a British fort. His wife, Elizabeth, was his nurse. She was allowed to take care of him. He was released from prison in 1781.

After the Americans won their independence, Thomas decided to work for the American government. He worked hard and was very dedicated. He became governor of South Carolina in 1787. He won the election with 163 votes out of 170. He served for two years.

In 1791, George Washington asked Pinckney to become a United States ambassador. President Washington wanted Pinckney to go to England to represent America. He would be the American ambassador, or official representative, to England. This was a difficult job. Many English officials were still upset with Americans over the Revolutionary War. Pinckney had to move there and work with these officials.

Chapter 4

Thomas and the Pinckney Treaty

In 1794, President Washington asked Pinckney to go to Spain. Thomas was to solve the argument between America and Spain. In his dealings with Spain, Pinckney was called the "extraordinary envoy." An envoy is a person who is sent as an official representative of a country.

Spain had great power in America. Spain controlled land to the south and west of the American states. Americans could not use the Gulf of Mexico and the Mississippi River. Spain stopped America from growing westward.

Pinckney arrived in Madrid, Spain, on June 28, 1795. He was greeted kindly by the Spanish court. Don Manuel de Godoy was in charge of working with Pinckney. De Godoy was also called Prince de la Paz. Pinckney wrote in his journal that de Godoy treated him fairly.

Pinckney did not use an interpreter. This was a challenge because he did not speak Spanish very well. He could, however, understand written Spanish. Don Manuel de Godoy understood spoken French. So Pinckney spoke French and de Godoy spoke Spanish. Pinckney disagreed with de Godoy about New Orleans. De Godoy granted Americans the right to use the Mississippi

This painting of Don Manuel de Godoy was created in the late eighteenth or early nineteenth century. De Godoy was given the title Prince de la Paz (prince of the peace) around 1795, after negotiating peace between France and Spain.

River, but he did not want to allow Americans to sell and ship goods in New Orleans. Eventually, de Godoy agreed to allow Americans to use New Orleans for three years. If the king of Spain was unhappy for any reason, he could forbid Americans from using New Orleans. If the Americans behaved well, the king would allow the Americans to build a port. The port would be on the bank of the Mississippi River, somewhere in Spanish territory.

Pinckney also wanted Spain to give back American goods and ships. These ships had been captured by Spain over many years. De Godoy refused. Pinckney told de Godoy that the meeting was over. Pinckney would not continue the meeting unless Spain agreed to the issue. The Spanish court decided to agree with Pinckney so that they could make a treaty.

A few other minor issues were settled over a few weeks. There were twenty-three articles, or rules, in the treaty. Pinckney and de Godoy signed the treaty on October 27, 1795. The treaty was given to the king. He approved it, and the treaty was sent to America. The

Long after Thomas Pinckney negotiated peace between the United States and Spain, the United States purchased the Louisiana Territory from France. In this illustration, a group of French settlers in Louisiana read a sign that explains that the French have surrendered the area to the United States. As their expressions show, the French were unhappy with the news.

- The United States's southern boundary was from the Atlantic Ocean to the Mississippi River along the 31st parallel. Spain could not claim land above the 31st parallel on the eastern side of the Mississippi River. Spain controlled the Florida and Louisiana Territories.

- Americans were allowed to use the Mississippi River, the Gulf of Mexico, and New Orleans.

- Problems between Americans and Spaniards would be settled in court. Americans and Spaniards were allowed to use each other's legal systems.

- Native Americans could not be asked to attack Spaniards or Americans. Neither country could use them to attack the other.

Senate approved the treaty, as did President Washington. The treaty then became law, and Thomas Pinckney became a hero in America. He was able to do what many could not. He made peace between Spain and America.

Because of the treaty, America was able to expand its territory westward. By 1802, Americans were bringing more than a million dollars worth of goods through New Orleans. The port made it easier to build new cities in the western frontier. Americans began to move into Spanish territories and western North America.

Ten years after Pinckney's Treaty, the Spanish and Americans had more arguments over land control. The American government purchased the Louisiana

Territory from France. The territory included some Spanish-controlled land. Americans rebelled against Spanish control. In 1819, the Spanish decided to give up their American claims. It was too expensive to fight off American growth in North America. The Spanish minister to America, Luis de Onís, signed the Adams-Onís Treaty. This gave Florida to the Americans ever after.

Glossary

ambassador (am-BA-suh-der) An official representative of one country who visits another country or who represents his or her country.

article (AR-ti-kuhl) A rule or law of a document or official paper.

colonist (KAH-luh-nist) A person who lives in a newly settled area.

colony (KAH-luh-nee) A territory that has been settled by people from another country. The colony is controlled by that country.

document (DOK-yoo-ment) A piece of paper or papers that contain important information.

envoy (ON-voy) A diplomat or official representative of a government, or a representative of a high-ranking official such as a king or president.

expand (ek-SPAND) To increase or grow in size.

foreign (FOR-in) Outside one's own country.

interpreter (in-TER-preht-er) Someone who helps people who speak different languages talk to each other.

plantation (plan-TAY-shun) A very large farm where crops are grown.

prosper (PRAHS-pur) To be successful or to thrive.

representative (reh-prih-ZEN-tuh-tiv) Someone who is chosen to act or speak for others.

resource (REE-sors) Something that is valuable or useful.

trade (TRAYD) The business of exchanging, buying, or selling goods.

treaty (TREE-tee) An official agreement between two or more countries.

Web Sites

Due to the changing nature of Internet links, the Rosen Publishing Group, Inc., has developed an online list of Web sites related to the subject of this book. This site is updated regularly. Please use this link to access the list:

http://www.rosenlinks.com/lnan/pitr

Primary Source Image List

Page 1: Panoramic map drawn by John Bachmann in 1861.
Page 4: Painting by J. Trumbull, engraved by W. G. Armstrong. Created in 1830. Housed in the South Caroliniana Library.
Page 9: Painting by Gilbert Stuart. Created in 1794. Lent by Peter A. Jay. On loan at the National Gallery of Art in Washington, DC
Page 11: The Treaty of Paris was created in 1783. Housed in the National Archives and Records Administration in Washington, DC.
Page 13: Map created by R. Sayer and J. Bennett in 1783.
Page 15: Map drawn by Anthony Nau, and engraved by Francis Shallus. Created in 1811.
Page 19: Undated painting of Charles Pinckney by Gilbert Stuart and Charles Fraser. Housed in the National Archives and Records Administration in Washington, DC.
Page 23: Painting by Esteve y Marqués. Housed in the Archivo Iconografico, S.A.

Index

A

Adams-Onís Treaty, 27
America, westward expansion of, 5, 6,
    11, 13–14, 22, 26
American colonies, independence of,
    9–11
American settlers, 6

E

England, 9–11, 12–13, 14, 18–21

F

Flint River, 15
Florida, 8, 9, 10, 11, 12, 14, 20, 26, 27
France, 6, 8, 9, 27

G

Gulf of Mexico, 8, 9, 12, 13, 14, 16,
    22, 26

J

Jay, John, 10

L

Louisiana Territory, 26, 27

M

Mississippi River, 8, 9, 10, 13, 14, 16,
    22–24, 26
    importance of, 12
Motte, Elizabeth, 20

N

Native Americans, 15, 16, 26
New Orleans, 8, 12, 14, 16, 23, 24, 26

O

Ohio River, 14
Onís, Luis de, 27

P

Paz, Prince de la (Don Manuel de
    Godoy), 5, 22–24
Pinckney, Charles, 18
Pinckney, Charles Cotesworth, 18
Pinckney, Elizabeth (Elizabeth Lucas),
    17–18
Pinckney, Thomas, 5, 16
    childhood and education
        of, 17–20
    as governor/ambassador, 20–21
    and negotiation of Pinckney Treaty,
        22–26

About the Author

Holly Cefrey is a freelance writer. Her books have been awarded a place on the *VOYA* 2001 Nonfiction Honor List. She is a member of the Authors Guild and the Society of Children's Book Writers and Illustrators.